NOV 1 5 2013

4/14   2015

W9-CPF-695

WHEN pets ATTACK!

SNAKES
ARE NOT PETS!

Gareth Stevens
Publishing

BY BARBARA LINDE

Dedication: For my writers group: Linda, Doris, Beverly, and Daria. Long may we critique!

Please visit our website, www.garethstevens.com. For a free color catalog of all our high-quality books, call toll free 1-800-542-2595 or fax 1-877-542-2596.

Library of Congress Cataloging-in-Publication Data

Linde, Barbara M.
Snakes are not pets! / by Barbara M. Linde.
   p. cm. — (When pets attack)
Includes index.
ISBN 978-1-4339-9299-5 (pbk.)
ISBN 978-1-4339-9300-8 (6-pack)
ISBN 978-1-4339-9298-8 (library binding)
1. Snakes as pets—Juvenile literature. 2. Reptiles as pets—Juvenile literature. I. Linde, Barbara M. II. Title.
SF459.S5 L56 2014
639.396—dc23

First Edition

Published in 2014 by
Gareth Stevens Publishing
111 East 14th Street, Suite 349
New York, NY 10003

Copyright © 2014 Gareth Stevens Publishing

Designer: Katelyn E. Reynolds
Editor: Therese Shea

Photo credits: Cover, pp. 1, 5 (image), 9, 21 iStockphoto/Thinkstock.com; cover, pp. 1–32 (home sweet home image) © iStockphoto.com/DNY59; cover, pp. 1–32 (background) Hemera/Thinkstock.com; cover, pp. 1–32 (blood splatter), pp. 3–32 (frame) iStockphoto/Thinkstock.com; p. 5 (map) Eightofnine/Wikipedia.com; p. 7 (diagram) Ned M. Seidler/ National Geographic/Getty Images; p. 7 (image) Design Pics/Thinkstock.com; pp. 8, 15 John Cancalosi/Peter Arnold/ Getty Images; p. 10 Chuck Rausin/Shutterstock.com; p. 11 Trahcus/Shutterstock.com; p. 12 Eric Isselee/Shutterstock.com; p. 13 (top) Ryan M. Bolton/Shutterstock.com; p. 13 (bottom) Patrick K. Campbell/Shutterstock.com; p. 17 Fletcher & Baylis/Photo Researchers/Getty Images; p. 19 Joe Raedle/Getty Images; p. 22 Yuril Cortez/AFP/Getty Images/ Getty Images; p. 23 Jaimie Duplass/Shutterstock.com; p. 25 Alexander Chelmodeev/Shutterstock.com; p. 27 Ruslan Semichev/Shutterstock.com; p. 29 Max Paddler/Gallo Images/Getty Images.

Printed in the United States of America

CPSIA compliance information: Batch #CS13GS: For further information contact Gareth Stevens, New York, New York at 1-800-542-2595.

CONTENTS

The Slithery Snake 4

Scaly Snake Bodies 6

Carnivores 10

Deadly Venomous Snakes 12

Gigantic Boas 14

Powerful Pythons 16

Pythons in the Everglades! 18

Snake Attacks 20

Snake Ownership 24

Snake Bacteria 26

Careers with Snakes .28

Glossary 30

For More Information .31

Index 32

Words in the glossary appear in **bold** type the first time they are used in the text.

THE SLITHERY SNAKE

They slither. They slide. They **shed**. They hiss. They're snakes! More than 2,700 kinds of snakes live on every continent except ice-cold Antarctica. Snakes vary in size. The tiniest ones are about 4 inches (10 cm) long, while the giants can grow to be 30 feet (9 m). Big and small, these wild animals are important to their natural **habitats**.

Some people keep snakes in their homes. However, snakes aren't cuddly, and they can't be trained. Snakes attack and kill prey. These are some reasons that snakes belong in the wild, not as pets. Are you curious to know more about them? Read on!

snake SAYINGS

Snakes are in some common sayings. A "snake in the grass" is a sneaky person who pretends to be a friend while acting in hurtful ways. If something is "snake oil," it's useless. Years ago, dishonest people sold liquids called snake oils. They were supposed to cure illnesses but never did.

Where Snakes Live

sea snakes
land snakes

Whether they live on land or in the water, snakes are fascinating creatures.

SCALY SNAKE BODIES

A snake has two eyes but no eyelids. Snakes don't have ear openings, but they do have inner ears. They can sense sounds in the air and through the ground. Some snakes make a hissing noise, but none have voices. They use a forked tongue to get information from smells, including where to find food.

Though a snake doesn't have any arms or legs, its long, tubelike shape helps it get around. The **vertebrae** in a snake's backbone allow it to move sideways and up and down. Its body is so **flexible** it can curl up in holes or wrap itself around trees—and prey.

snakes IN STORIES

People's interest in snakes is reflected in the many snake characters in fiction books. In *The Jungle Book* by Rudyard Kipling, Kaa is a powerful python. J. K. Rowling created Nagini, an evil snake in the *Harry Potter* series. Asmodeus Poisonteeth is an adder in *Redwall* by Brian Jacques.

lung

eyes

vertebrae

heart

forked tongue

stomach

Snakes come in many colors and often
blend in with their surroundings.

As a molting snake wriggles along the ground, it leaves its old, see-through skin behind, usually in one piece!

8

In the TV series *Lego Ninjago: Masters of Spinjitzu*, the heroes fight evil tribes of snakes. Sir Hiss is the prince's sinister assistant in Disney's movie *Robin Hood*. Not all snakes are bad in stories, though. In *Kung Fu Panda*, Master Viper is a green snake. She's kind and a great dancer.

Scales cover the snake's entire body—even its eyes. Dry, dead scales form from the outer layer of skin. They feel hard, like your fingernails. The skin between the scales stretches. This is how a snake can swallow a large animal.

Many times during its lifetime, a snake molts, or sheds its outer skin. The snake scratches its head on something rough to get the skin loose. It crawls headfirst out of the old skin. The inner layer of skin becomes the outer layer. If you owned a snake, you'd have to clean up its old skin!

shed snake skin

CARNIVORES

All snakes are **carnivores**. Many snakes don't chase after their prey though. Instead, they hide. When an unsuspecting animal comes near, the snake **lunges** forward to grab it. It uses its strong jaws and sharp teeth to hold on to its prey. A snake's jaws and entire body can stretch so it can slowly swallow its meal.

All snakes have teeth, and some have **fangs** full of venom. When they bite their prey, the venom enters the animal's body. Other snakes are constrictors. They wrap tightly around their prey and squeeze their muscles, or constrict, until their victims can't breathe.

venom

Venom is a poison that a snake makes inside its body. It travels through tubelike **ducts** into the fangs. When the snake bites, the fangs pierce the prey's skin, and the venom flows into the animal. Some types of venom make the prey stop moving. Others kill it.

Most people don't want carnivorous pets—or dangerous ones!

DEADLY VENOMOUS SNAKES

The eastern diamondback rattlesnake lives in the southeastern United States. It doesn't strike at people unless it has been startled or teased, but its venom is very painful and can kill.

Eastern coral snakes also live in the Southeast. Their bite doesn't seem painful at first, but the venom works slowly. If not treated, a bitten person can die from heart or lung failure.

The king cobra is native to India, south China, and Southeast Asia. Reaching lengths of 18 feet (5.5 m) from head to tip, it's the longest venomous snake. It can spread out its hooded head to look even bigger. A king cobra's bite can kill an elephant!

snakebite!

If a venomous snake bites you, you'll need immediate medical help. The treatment will probably include antivenin. Antivenin is a medicine made from venom that can stop the effects of the poison. Bites from nonvenomous snakes can cause dangerous **infections** and need many stitches, too.

king cobra

These snakes would make some of the worst pets of all!

eastern diamondback rattlesnake

eastern coral snake

GIGANTIC BOAS

Boas are a group of constrictor snakes. They live on several continents but mainly in warm, **tropical** parts of Central and South America. Boas live in trees, on land, and sometimes underground.

Green anacondas, a type of boa, live in South American rainforests. Other snakes may be slightly longer, but not heavier. Green anacondas can weigh up to 550 pounds (250 kg). That's too big to get around easily on land, so these boas glide through rivers and streams. Anacondas aren't poisonous, but they're dangerous constrictors. Their jaws open so wide, they can swallow a whole deer!

how snakes ARE BORN

Most snakes hatch from eggs. The mother lays them in a hole in the ground or another hidden place. She may wrap, or coil, her body around the eggs to protect them, or leave them. However, boas give birth to live baby snakes. As soon as the snakes are born, they leave the mother.

Green Anacondas' Range

South America

where green
anacondas live

A boa constrictor is pictured here with its young.

POWERFUL PYTHONS

Pythons are mostly found in Australia, Africa, and Asia. Two kinds of pythons can grow to be 30 feet (9 m) long—the African rock python and the reticulated (rih-TIH-kyuh-lay-tuhd) python. You don't want one of these in your living room!

Like boas, pythons are constrictors. They're great swimmers, so they spend a lot of time in the water. A python might swim along with its huge body underwater and its head peeking out. It looks for birds, lizards, and other small animals. As soon as prey comes close enough, the python strikes!

threatened

Pythons and boas are being taken from their natural habitats. Hunters go after them for their beautiful skins or to sell them to pet shops. Some people even eat them. The snakes' habitats are also being torn down for wood and building space. Several countries protect snakes, such as the Burmese python, so they won't die out.

Pythons have a variety of colorful skin patterns.

PYTHONS IN THE EVERGLADES!

Burmese pythons aren't native to the Florida Everglades, but they're a big problem there. Scientists think thousands of pythons are slithering around the swampy land. It's similar to their natural habitat. The pythons have plenty of prey, including birds, squirrels, deer—and even alligators!

How did the pythons get into the Everglades? Many owners couldn't handle the huge snakes, so they put them there. Some pythons also escaped from pet stores damaged during hurricanes.

The government is afraid the pythons will soon spread to other areas. One captured mother python had just laid 85 eggs when they found her!

the python PATROL

The Nature Conservancy trains **volunteers** to look for pythons in the Everglades. If they see a python, they call a special telephone number. Wildlife specialists come to the place and capture the snake. Some volunteers are trained to capture the snakes. They hold them until the specialists arrive.

Pythons are eating many animals in the Everglades and threatening other animals' ways of life. Pythons are either removed or killed when they're found.

SNAKE ATTACKS

Large snakes make especially dangerous pets. Such a snake can push through a screen or door, or knock the top off a cage that isn't locked properly. Once a snake coils around someone, it may be too powerful to remove.

A 13-foot (4 m) python killed its 19-year-old owner in his apartment in New York City. The police found the snake wrapped around him. They think the young man took the snake out of its cage to feed it because there was a live chicken in a box in the apartment. The snake probably mistook the young man for prey.

too many ATTACKS

According to the Humane Society of the United States, constrictor snakes have killed at least 17 people in the past 35 years. Many people have survived nasty bites, too. These people were in their homes and gardens, at parties, and in pet shops. Even snake experts have been attacked while showing snakes in schools or parks.

A snake like this could easily squeeze the breath out of a person.

Large snakes belong in cages in museums, nature centers, or—even better—in their natural habitat.

not-so-friendly NEIGHBORS

When big snakes get out, they threaten the whole neighborhood. A python attacked a man in his garden. One snake escaped from a car and wounded a little girl. A python hid under a minivan and lashed out at a man getting into the car. Snakes don't have to be big or long to do damage.

One snake got out of its cage and hid in a dresser drawer. When a young boy opened the drawer, the snake bit him. Many snake owners have been bitten when they put their hands inside cages. Snakes sometimes wander from homes. Even pet shop employees and wildlife experts get attacked sometimes.

There are several terrible stories of snakes attacking—and even killing—children after escaping from their cages. Parents have been sent to jail for not protecting their children from dangerous pets. Some of these snakes were just 1 foot (30 cm) long when purchased, so people thought they were harmless.

SNAKE OWNERSHIP

Though the US Humane Society doesn't support keeping snakes as pets, many people still do. These people need to answer many important questions: Is the snake's tank big enough? Is the temperature comfortable for it? Do they have enough live or frozen animals to feed the snake? Do they have enough money to buy food and other supplies? Is it even legal to own the snake they have or want?

Garter or rough green snakes are safer choices for snake owners. These snakes don't grow any longer than your arm. They eat earthworms, bugs, or small fish.

laws for PET OWNERS

The US government doesn't allow people to bring Burmese pythons and some other large snakes into the United States. In some states, it's illegal to own dangerous snakes. Others require a permit. The laws protect the pet owners, their neighbors, and the snakes.

A pet snake needs a large terrarium, a tank that looks and feels like its natural habitat. Without the proper terrarium, a snake won't stay healthy.

SNAKE BACTERIA

Do you know most snakes carry **bacteria** called salmonella in their bodies? Since you can't see the bacteria, you can't know if a snake is infected with it. The snakes don't get sick from the bacteria, but they can pass it on to people.

If you handle a snake, touch something it has touched, or clean its cage, wash your hands thoroughly. Most people get very sick from salmonella poisoning, but some have even died. The Centers for Disease Control report over 93,000 people every year get salmonella from reptiles like snakes and turtles.

sick SNAKES

Snakes can get sick, especially in **captivity**. They get skin **diseases** and can have breathing problems. They may not be able to shed properly or rid themselves of their waste. Some snakes get cancer, too. Not every veterinarian can help with sick snakes.

Bacteria are easily passed from a snake's skin to yours. Wash your hands carefully with soap and water after touching a snake.

CAREERS WITH SNAKES

The Humane Society thinks snakes should stay in the wild. If you like snakes, why not turn your interest into a career? You could become a **herpetologist**. You might teach or conduct studies about snakes. National and state wildlife agencies hire herpetologists. They go into the field to check on the health and habitats of snake populations.

Zoo workers take care of snake exhibits. They may take snakes to schools. Other snake experts write books or give talks about snakes. You could even be a wildlife photographer and capture images of snakes in the wild for magazines!

studying SNAKES

To become a herpetologist, you'll need to take many kinds of science classes. You'll also need classes in math and English. Be prepared to go to college for about 4 years. More education may be needed after that depending on what you want to do.

Herpetologists travel all over the world to find snakes.

GLOSSARY

bacteria: tiny creatures that can only be seen with a microscope

captivity: the state of being caged

carnivore: an animal that eats meat

disease: illness

duct: a tubelike passage in the body through which fluid passes

fang: a long, pointed tooth

flexible: able to bend easily

habitat: the natural place where an animal or plant lives

herpetologist: someone who studies reptiles and amphibians

infection: a sickness caused by germs

lunge: a sudden forward motion

shed: to lose fur or skin

tropical: having to do with the warm parts of Earth near the equator

vertebrae: the small bones that make up the backbone

volunteer: a person who works without being paid

FOR MORE INFORMATION

Books

Gibbons, Gail. *Snakes.* New York, NY: Holiday House, 2010.

Simon, Seymour. *Poisonous Snakes.* Mineola, NY: Dover Publications, 2012.

Stewart, Melissa. *Snakes!* Washington, DC: National Geographic, 2009.

Websites

Photo Gallery: Snakes
animals.nationalgeographic.com/animals/photos/snakes/
Read the description of a snake and view a photo of it. Watch a video interview with a herpetologist.

Snakes of North America
www.pitt.edu/~mcs2/herp/SoNA.html
Find out what kinds of snakes live near you!

INDEX

antivenin 12

attacks 4, 20, 23

bacteria 26, 27

boas 14, 15, 16

carnivores 10, 11

colors 7, 17

constrictors 10, 14, 15, 16, 20

diseases 26

eastern coral snake 12, 13

eastern diamondback
    rattlesnake 12, 13

eggs 14, 18

Everglades 18, 19

eyes 6, 7, 9

fangs 10

green anacondas 14, 15

habitats 4, 16, 18, 22, 25, 28

herpetologists 28, 29

hissing 4, 6

inner ears 6

king cobra 12

molting 8, 9

movies and TV 9

prey 4, 10, 16, 18, 20

pythons 6, 16, 17, 18, 19, 20, 23,
    24

salmonella 26

scales 9

shed 4, 9, 26

skin 8, 9, 10, 16, 17, 26, 27

snakebites 10, 12, 20, 23

snake sayings 4

snakes in books 6

teeth 10

tongue 6, 7

venom 10, 12